ONLINE INCON

BEGINNER'S GUIDE TO MAKING PASSIVE MONEY WITH ONLINE BUSINESS (AMAZON, EBAY, WEB DESIGN, SHOPIFY, SECRET STRATEGIES)

Descrierea CIP a Bibliotecii Naționale a României
PARKER, GREG
   Online income : beginner's guide to making passive money
with online business / by Greg Parker. - București : My Ebook,
2018
   ISBN 978-606-983-615-6

336

ONLINE INCOME

BEGINNER'S GUIDE TO MAKING PASSIVE
MONEY WITH ONLINE BUSINESS
(AMAZON, EBAY, WEB DESIGN, SHOPIFY,
SECRET STRATEGIES)

My Ebook Publishing House
Bucharest, 2018

CONTENTS

INTRODUCTION

I want to thank you and congratulate you for buying the book, ***Online Income: Beginner's Guide To Making Passive Money With Online Business.***

This book contains proven steps and strategies for making money online. I assure that this book would equip your mind and give you reasons why remaining poor is your choice – No Excuse. The e-commerce in 2017 was valued at $2.3 trillion and in 2021 it is projected to reach $4.5 trillion, that's a lot of money just to sit idle and watch go by, we have to take active steps to position ourselves to harness this wealth pool. That's why I am writing this book, I hope to help you bridge the missing gaps and inspire you to achieve your financial goals for your life.

Join me on a ride as I show you easy steps to getting rich, by using your handy tech devices and available online platforms. Start smiling!

CHAPTER ONE

THE ONLINE MARKET SPACE AND ITS BENEFITS

With the advent of the internet and the creation of social media, the world has been altered significantly as it has to do with business. A lot of businesses moved online, and it affected our brick and mortar shopping systems. People now shop online with almost no effort and get their goods delivered to their doorsteps. This was possible due to the heavy influx of millions of internet users daily. Technology is subtly changing how we interact with one another, from our languages to our trends, to our body languages; everything is affected by the huge wave of internet users. According to Wikipedia, 47% of the world's population are internet users, as of 2005, we had only 16% of the world's population. That's an amazing increase and it is projected that by 2020 there would be up to 4.1 billion users of internet worldwide that's over 52% of the world's population. That's actually a new market space in one location – online! The internet is one big market space.

Let's not even begin to look into the development of devices that enable internet access: from android phones to laptops, to Private computers, etc. all these inventions make it easier to access the internet. Developers of social media sites have learnt how to keep people glued to their social media platforms, with constant interactions: sharing, liking, and posting. Just last year Facebook recorded 2.07 billion active monthly users and over 1 billion active daily mobile users; while on Instagram, they record over 500 million users daily; Pinterest also records 150 million active users; Google records about 40,000 searches per second and 3.5billion searches every day. These alarming stats are why digital marketers and social media influencers are making so much money on the internet. Businesses began to harness this online market, full of "click" addicted folks. Online ads shot up the roof. The online space has become saturated; more people online means the smart way to make money quickly would be to join the online market space as fast as possible.

The advent of online shopping is another brilliant idea that has swept the market space. Online marketers and shoppers make and spend millions of dollars monthly. The largest online retail store is Amazon, and you can buy almost everything there, from clothes to books, to technological items, etc. the largeness of the online market space is growing daily like a black hole and sucking in all the cash, as of 2014 the internet space contributed 966.6 billion dollars to the GDP of the U.S economy. The world has gone digital. A lot of things we know now are going obsolete, like physical fliers are replaced by e-fliers, cable TV by Netflix and YouTube and so many other things. The ecommerce in 2017 was valued at $2.3 trillion and in 2021 it is projected to reach $4.5 trillion, that's a lot of money to just sit idle and watch go by, we have to take active steps to position ourselves to harness this wealth pool.

TOOLS AND PLATFORMS THAT ENABLE YOU MAKE MONEY ONLINE FAST

There are tools and online platforms that you can easily log into and make money quickly. We would dedicate the next chapters to explain the steps and strategies.

Here are the platforms, we would consider:

AMAZON

EBAY

WEB DESIGN

SHOPIFY

CHAPTER TWO

HOW TO MAKE MONEY ON AMAZON

(1) Amazon is currently the largest online retail store in the world, and they launched a new platform called "**Amazon associates or Amazon affiliates**". Amazon Affiliates, get an incentive (about 4-10% of the purchase) when people click on the links available on their sites. These links lead customers to the Amazon site where they purchase their items and the associate gets paid for it.

How to become an Amazon affiliate?

• Build a website: you'd have to buy a domain. Get a good domain name positions you for better SEO (search engine optimization). It makes it easy for your customers to find you online and doesn't get people confused about your site – a unique domain name is tantamount. Also, get and set up hosting. You'd have to set up a website that meets the Amazon standard requirements. These requirements would be provided during the Amazon affiliate program as not just any website qualifies. It is also imperative that affiliates state clearly, what the terms and conditions of doing business on their website are. This is a required condition.

• Carve a niche (sector): one of the reasons why people don't make so much impact in their businesses is because they are lost in the market space; no one can say what they are all about. It is important that you are clear in your mind and your business perspective about the work you are doing and where your market is. You need to carve out space. In the vastness of the Amazon world, 'keywords' are your keys to navigation and easily finding the product you want. If you don't carve a niche for yourself, since you are a mini website, customers would go to Amazon directly to purchase. If you are specialised in an area, you become the authority and the go-to-guy for that particular product or brand. You can carve a niche by researching areas with less competition, areas where customers would naturally flow towards, is it possible that you can be an affiliate in the niche you have chosen, your passion.

- Get ready to get traffic: it would be dumb to just have a website and get Amazon to accept you as an associate and not, have traffic or people who would purchase the product you are offering. You would have to get traffic. If you are an already established blogger with huge traffic in your blog or you have a website and you churn out content that attracts huge traffic you are good to go, but if you don't, you'd have to instigate processes that would attract the right traffic to your website. One of the best ways of getting traffic to your site is if you have interesting content. Content ranges from, theme to attractive pictures and compelling stories. Whatever you do, make sure your content is up to date and at the edge of your game. You also must be consistent with all the content you are churning out, it helps build customer loyalty and customer trust. They will keep coming if they know they would get content from you. It generates and keeps traffic on your site.

- Use powerful advertisement: no one will come to you if they don't know you exist. So get word out there. The best platform to advertise will be online. Utilise the social media space (social media marketing and ads) they provide a stream lined and properly targeted market for your exploitation. You could also use social media influencers. These guys already have traction on the internet, and are strongly influencing culture, if you can afford it, they can help increase traffic on your site. Direct Email Marketing (DEM) is another great way to get the word out there. Get a couple of emails and send them links with a little description about your site. There are organisations that can help you do this.

(2) SELL DIRECTLY ON AMAZON: another way you can make money on Amazon is to sell directly on Amazon. Just identify the products that are in demand, check out for the Amazon's check list, fulfil the check list, upload your product on Amazon, take really catchy pictures of your product, describe your product and you are good to go. If you don't have products to sell, you can be a middle-middle man between people who have these products and help them sell online on Amazon. You get an incentive and you pay your suppliers.

Amazon also has other platforms like:

Amazon reviews: where you get paid for giving honest reviews about Amazon products; Amazon Mechanical Turk etc.

(3) PUBLISH EBOOKS AND ORIGINAL CONTENT: this is another medium to churn out income from Amazon, if you are a writer, write eBooks and give them titles that are keywords in searches on Amazon. It helps your books to be found amidst the mass of eBooks on Amazon. Also consistently develop personal content on Amazon and upload them.

CHAPTER THREE

HOW TO MAKE MONEY AS A Web Designer

Web design is the creation and maintenance of websites. Web designing is a skill that is built on other skills like, graphic design; interface design; content development, motion graphics, including standardised code and proprietary software; user experience design; and search engine optimization (SEO).

Creation of websites drags in so much income for the person who has the skills, and it is really not that hard, just have to get the necessary tools and steps on how to create and manage a website.

(1) KNOW YOUR JOB: the first step for me is to know what you are doing. No client would want to pay you for a job that is not well known. Get conversant with the work you are doing. Get so good at it, that any customer you work for would have no other choice but to give you a 5star rating. Web designing and creation is a very lucrative job if the web designing knows his job. Get as much training as possible. There are online platforms and physical training centres. Get trained, get more skills as the information world is evolving, if you don't keep up, you might become obsolete. You can add software development skills too...

(2) MAKE YOURSELF AVAILABLE: what's the use having a great skill and customers can't reach you? It is important that you are always out there and available to do great jobs.

(3) MAKE YOUR SOCIAL MEDIA HANDLES YOUR ONLINE RESUME: it is important to know that social media is a platform that can enable you be visible in real time. Turn your social media handle to an online resume. Post your work, write great content–you don't know who is watching. Most of the web designers I know got their major jobs off the social media. That's like your platform to show the world what you can do. Pay more attention to professional sites like linkedIn.

(4) REACH OUT TO YOUR CLIENTS: as much as we agree that your social media handles can be your online curriculum vitae, some of your potential customers might not be on social media or might not be able to see your work. Write very detailed proposals and/with demos of your work and forward it to them. Reach out to local small businesses; get them to see reasons why they need a website and the value they would bring to their businesses.

(5) WATCH OUT FOR REFERRALS: one of the fastest ways to sell your brand as a designer is by referral. That's why it is so important you do your job well, if not you won't get good referral from clients. It is good to execute jobs that hit the excellent mark

and deliver customer satisfaction. Makes sure after a job, you get the clients to talk about your works, either on your website or on other platforms; maybe the platform they reached you through, but either way, Referrals are important!

(6) NETWORK: if you are a freelance, you might find other freelancers around who have a strong brand in the market and as a result of that, they have clients trooping in for their services, because they are freelance, they might easily pass the job on to you. Form a strong network of web designers: make sure, you know who is who in the business. It helps you keep track on what's trending in the markets because you are a greenhorn and are not conversant with the market space like the older designers.

(7) DON'T THROW CONTACTS AWAY: after you do business with a client, always stay in touch. Don't discard the clients contact. Learn to stay in touch. You can do this, by sending them personalised emails asking them of how they loved your product and if you could still be of help. If you did a good job, recalling you won't be a problem.

(8) CARVE A NICHE: this is important, although you can do what virtually all web designers can, but have a specialty that would set you apart from the rest of your competition, whether it is your unique ability to give very good SEOs or your ability to give them outstanding themes, or outstanding content, whatever it is, always stand out. Give your work a little bit of an accent.

(9) TURN IT INTO A BUSINESS: as you become popular and your brand becomes stronger, you'd have more clients, it would be a terrible idea to turn down a lot of jobs. The more you turn them down, they would turn to your competitors and you'd lose potential customers. Create a business out of it: hire staff, get an office, get registered, aim for bigger jobs, and expand the vision of what's possible.

(10) BUILD YOUR CLIENTELE: gradually build your clientele. It's Important you have and build a list of your customers for testimonials and referrals.

(11) JOIN FREELANCING SITES: freelancing sites are sites where you

subscribe to, showcase your work and bid for jobs. These sites have a heavy traction and customers are sure to find a web designer there. The only set back with these platforms are that you already have designers that have high ratings and attract more jobs. You'd have to think of a creative way to attract customers to you.

(12) PRICE PROPERLY: pricing can either attract the right customer or, repel them, that's why using the proper pricing systems are imperative to attracting clients as a beginner.

Being a web designer is a fun way to make money especially if you are very creative and innovative. The best kind of work to do is work you enjoy doing. It's not all about just doing the work; you also have to pay attention to the business of web designing. What that means is, as you focus on having fun, you also focus on making money, and that would take discipline and focus. This is the only way you can move from making small digit incomes, to six digit income. You have to make the business out of your work as a designer. Most importantly, you have to be consistent...let me paraphrase, you have to consistently give add and give value. This is what the clients would come back for. They would come back for the value they got, to keep them glued, give them something better so you must always look for exiting ways to make your customers satisfied and happy. If you apply these principles you would do well as a designer.

CHAPTER FOUR

HOW TO MAKE MONEY ON eBay

EBay is an e-commerce corporation with its head office in San Jose California and is found in different countries around the world. EBay caries out transactions between one consumer and another; and between one business and its consumer's sales through its website. EBay was created by Pierre Omidyar in 1995, and became a very successful web story. Now, eBay is worth billions of dollars and is found in over 30 countries of the world. EBay has a website called eBay.com, a site where they sell any item and rake in loads of buyers. EBay has created opportunities for people worldwide to transact and buy products of their choice. There are a lot of ways of making money on EBay, sellers and buyers are profiting from eBay online sales. This is a profitable venture for anyone who wants to make money online fast. The eBay policies are customer and seller friendly. People can shop and buy anything on eBay.

Why eBay? It is fast, doesn't cost much, and there are already a stream of buyers on eBay (over 152 million active users on eBay).

To start up with eBay, you simply have to have an eBay account. Register on the eBay site and get an account, this account enables you to sell or buy anything on the site. You also need a very attractive user ID, nothing ambiguous; try using simple and memorable

IDs. The next thing to do is also get a PAY PAL account, where your funds are transferred to after transaction success. PayPal enables your customers to make use of a credit card or make use of a checking account to purchase the items. It also provides you the platform for selling internationally. Customers kick start the payment process with PayPal, and PayPal, pays the money into your account when the transaction is complete.

You would also have to decide what to sell, If not you might be lost in the vast cloud of "the online market". There are a lot of sellers and selling activities ongoing on eBay. Also do an online tour around eBay, see what others are selling, what is trending, what product is on high demand and their prices, it would help you fix the best price for your product. I would also suggest you do some buying on eBay first, see how it works, know if you can handle the heat. You also have to know how to describe your product, so that the customer has an idea of what he is buying and its value. Take nice photos, that enable your customer see what he is buying, the more convincing the photos are, and the more the chances are of sealing the deal.

There are ways of marketing your product on eBay (create you listings): **BY AUCTION**. When you list your items for auction, you open it for a bid between customers and buyers and it depends on if the product meets customer interest. You set a number of days where the customers or buyers to bid for the product. The highest bid is the selling price for your product. EBay statistics say, people buy auctioned items more.

Another way is **THE RESERVE METHOD**: when you list items for auction, they can be auctioned and priced for prices that are not favourable to you, you can set a minimum bid price that your product could go for. It is a safe way of getting paid for your auctioned item without the price going below the value of the product auctioned or listed. There is a fee paid for adding reserve prices to your auction listing, but it's a safe bet. This option might not be the best for beginners that might not know the pricing wave on eBay yet.

Another listing option is the **BUY IT NOW** method: The Buy it now option, lets you set a price for your product right from the time you listed the product. Buyers see your price and can decide to purchase. The price is sort of fixed from the beginning and the customer sees this price once he views your product. The Buy It Now option, allows you to sell your item quickly for your chosen price.

EBay offers you options on listings and how to market your item on its site. Fo through and find which option best suites you.

When on eBay, you would have to watch your pricing. This is very important as you have other people on eBay selling almost similar products with you, your price needs to be very attractive and reasonable. Don't over price, if not you would drive customers away. EBay has standard and general pricing options, you could check those pricing options on the eBay site.

When a transaction is concluded, a review should be left online to let others know what it is like to do business on eBay. I would suggest that you encourage your customers to leave a review of how the transaction you had with them was. The better testimonials you compound the better your chance of increasing your customer base. One of the best ways to advertise a business, is by word of mouth. Let your customers, bring you other customers with their reviews.

Customer service also comes to play, it determines how you relate with customers and how you can convince them to buy your product. It's a skill every business person should have.

Here are a few platforms to make money on EBay:

(1) EBAY'S AFFILIATE PROGRAM: if you want to make money on eBay without having what to sell, this is the best option for you. EBay provides a platform for people to earn money online from its "online market place" without actually selling or having products to sell. EBay's affiliate program provides access for online publishers and content makers to direct traffic to eBay and earn money.

EBay's affiliate platform enables content makers to earn money by encouraging ecommerce traders. Content makers, can harness existing web traffic, how? They refer web visitors to their merchant associates through unique and tractable links. When a purchase is made by the referred customer, you can get an incentive. EBay's Partner Network (EPN) is an internal affiliate program and has a plethora of exciting options for people to (publishers) to partake and earn money from. The platform provides content publishers with tools to monetize their websites, social media handles, apps, and every online corridor available to the content publisher by converting people visiting their sites to potential buyers on eBay and eventually customers.

To sign up for eBay's partner's network, you need to establish a presence on the internet. That means you have to have traffic on your web platform. Before even thinking of traffic you have to have a website (simple steps to create a website are listed above). You must have generated good traffic on your web platform with your good and consistent content, in fact, what you need is an available market (traffic) that would buy from eBay. Once that is done, you need to sign up to eBay's partner's network this doesn't even take much time, the time that you'd spend to create an eBay's partner's network depends on you and how prepared you are.

Once you are accepted, you will receive access to items and options that you can add to your website or social media. If you are a novice, you can just copy and paste the code to your web platform. It is an easy to do process for beginners and novices, to get started with. If you are not a novice and have more skills in development, you can access the eBay's API; this enables you to create more custom made solutions. Just like Amazon, you have to carve a niche for yourself on the kind of products you want to promote and categories you have the market for. You need to study your traffic to understand the kind of categories and product to focus on. Do not shoot without aim. Focus is key to success.

If you run a website that focused on technology, it would not be smart to promote a category that focused on clothes, except they are clothes that have a lot to do with technology, like safety gears. Why? Because your audience is tech savvy and are interested in technology. They would only respond to items and content to appeal to their interests. So know your audience and choose a category that would appeal to them.

Then you create so much content and ads about the product you are selling, the better you are able to convince them, the better the chances are that you would be patronised.

A lot of people buy items not because they know the product, but simply because of word of mouth. If you are a social media influencer or you have large followership on the internet, you can begin to write reviews about products on eBay that you are promoting. Certain eBay sellers and store owners can contact you to promote their work or write reviews for them if you already have high traffic on your site and a strong influence over your audience. This would be another source of income for you. Your reviews should be well researched, honest views on items on eBay, this would draw buyers to your site, and hence you get paid for purchases and listings. You can make a full time job out of this, just learn the basic skills and go for it!

(2) OPEN AN EBAY STORE: eBay stores are a unique section in eBay that enables individual sellers to display all the products they have for sale. The eBay store helps the sellers describe and engage customers about their businesses through the pages they have customised and the brand they have created on eBay. A door icon can be seen next to a seller's user ID which is to show that the seller already possess an eBay Store, and with one click the buyer gains access into your store and can go through the options and items available in the store. The eBay store options provides the seller the

opportunity to take advantage of the store to advance their business on eBay. They have access to cheap, easy to manoeuvre tools that enable the seller build their brand which in turn will increase patronage.

How can I open one?

• To start an eBay store you need to meet the seller's requirements, have an eBay account, a verified PayPal account, to advance to other options available for eBay stores, you would need to be up to your game and progress.

• After you meet the requirements, you need to subscribe to eBay store. Scroll through the subscription options and pick one that suits you, your budget and what you want to do. Then pick a name for your store, an easy to remember name or store title that would make your store easy to spot. Names help to create strong brand identity. You need to be different from your competition and one of the ways is to have a unique name. This name will determine your stores URL.

Subscribe to eBay Stores

- It's now time to go aesthetical; you would have to design your store and arrange the necessary tools. You have to choose a good theme, colour and make your store look so unique and easy for customers (buyers) to navigate your store. Try to give your store a professional look; this would increase the chances of patronage and eventually growing brand loyalty (that means having customers come back again, and again). Make sure you check the rules governing eBay's stores so you would not do something against eBay's rule of handling a store.

Finally, list your items, manage your store, and promote your store. Do anything possible to get the store out there and selling!

CHAPTER FIVE

HOW TO MAKE MONEY THROUGH SHOPIFY

We have come to the final platform we have chosen to talk about. Shopify is an online website and ecommerce platform that enables you set your own online store from any location and start selling your items on the platform. Shopify has helped businesses rake thousands and even millions by just interacting online with buyers and sellers.

Why Shopify? Shopify is an easy to handle internet e-commerce platform. They have tools that help you easily navigate through to build your online store. Shopify is a reliable online market platform.

How to use Shopify:

To start a Shopify store, you have to check out which of the store categories you want and fit your budget as all Shopify stores are paid for. After you have chosen your store plan and paid for it, you need to organise your store. Shopify provides you with features that are very interesting and can help you create an appealing and professional looking store. Added to the Shopify list of features, it has the 'mobile responsiveness' option that enables clients to reach your store via their android phones.

If you already have a company with staff, Shopify provides your staff opportunity to be involved. It is just like your office with staff, but the difference with this one is that it is online. You can set levels of permission for your staff. They also can access the Shopify platform. It allows you to have an oversight of your company, whether online or offline.

You should already know what you want to sell on Shopify. It's not wise to venture into a business without any proper plan and your niche well defined. It matters a lot to be very distinct from your competition, and there is no better way than studying them and through their weakness create a niche from which your business would thrive. So it's important you already know what you want to sell.

Shopify also helps you manage, SEO (search engine optimization). What's the point of doing something and no one sees you? Shopify handles it by using specific key words, Meta tags, and site maps so that when anyone searches anything that resembles what you do, your website is easily accessed. Shopify also provides other benefits including access to email marketing. Shopify integrates with other social media platforms for visibility. Also, it integrates with other e-commerce sites like eBay and Amazon. There are many features available for you to choose and use. You can also become a Shopify affiliate; Shopify partner; Shopify expert and authority, where you educate Shopify stores on how to run their stores, promote them and use the Shopify tools to maximise business success. You can engage in drop shipping on Shopify where a buyer pays for a product you don't have; you go to the vendor that has it buy it and ship it to the buyer and take your profit. Shopify does not need an extra payment channel like

PayPal; it has its own transactional security. Shopify is a good option for e-commerce.

CONCLUSION

The online market is a place to be. You can harness the myriad of opportunities available to the market space and earn a lot of money. You just need common sense, the right tools, and the right skills. This book has provided the tools required to at least get you started. It is time to get to work.

Thank you again for purchasing this book! I hope this book was able to equip you with necessary tools to make money online fast. The next step like I said earlier is to get to work.

Finally, if you enjoyed this book, then I'd like to ask you a favour, would you be kind enough to leave a review for this book? It'd be greatly appreciated!

Thank you and good luck!